BUILDING BUSINESS 4 SUCCESS

THE DEFINITIVE GUIDE TO STARTING AND GROWING YOUR BUSINESS FOR A PROFITABLE FUTURE

WALT CAMPING

Copyright ©Walt Camping 2015 & 2019:
All Rights Reserved

This Book is copyrighted. No part of this Book may be reproduced, stored in a retrieval system, or transmitted by any other means: electronic, mechanical, photocopying, recording, or otherwise, without prior written permission of the copyright holders.

This Book is supplied for information purposes only and, as experienced in this subject matter as the contributors are, the material herein does not constitute professional advice.

This Book is designed to provide accurate and authoritative information with regard to the subject matter covered. It is sold with the understanding that the publisher and the contributors are not engaged in rendering legal, accounting, or other professional advice.

If legal advice or other professional assistance is required, the services of a competent professional should be sought.

The reader is advised to consult with an appropriately qualified professional before making any business decision. The contributor, Walt Camping, do not accept any responsibility for any liabilities resulting from the business decisions made by purchasers of this book.

*EARNINGS DISCLAIMER: Results are not typical. Your results may vary. We make no claim that you will earn any income using this Book whatsoever.

Where specific figures are quoted from individuals there is no assurance you will do as well.

You must assume the risk that you will not earn any income from this product.

CONTENTS

Foreword v
Introduction ix

Chapter 1 - Why do Businesses Fail?   1
Chapter 2 - It's All About the Hats You Wear   11
Chapter 3 - The Hat of Knowledge   15
Chapter 4 - The Management & Administration Hat   19
Chapter 5 - The Technical Hat   27
Chapter 6 - The Planner's Hat   31
Chapter 7 - The Salesman's Hat   37
Chapter 8 - The Hat of Servitude   57
Chapter 9 - The Financial Hat   63
Chapter 10 - The Legal Hat   69
Chapter 11 - It's a Capital Hat!   73
Chapter 12 - The Retiree's Hat   81
Chapter 13 - The Learner's Hat   85
Chapter 14 - The Spy's Hat   89
Chapter 15 – Putting it All Together – Your Business, Your Future   95

FOREWORD

I received a call from my good friend, Walt Camping. He asked if we could meet because he had something he wanted to share with me. We met at a nice cafe on Camelback Road in Phoenix, AZ. It was a perfectly sunny 70-degree day. About 30 minutes into just getting caught up, Walt pulled a neat stack of papers out of his briefcase. He handed them to me and said . . . 'Here's my new book!' He asked me if I would write the Forward to the book. For a moment I was speechless. Walt is not only a good friend, but also a great businessman. His talent for building and running successful businesses is unsurpassed. Anyone thinking about or planning to launch or run a company should read this book in its total.

I have had the good fortune of knowing Walt since he was just getting started building his most recent company, observing on the inside as an investor. Walt makes great decisions and choices. He knows what he is doing. I have found that if I want to do something well, I must find someone who has done it and learn from them. This is your opportunity to learn from someone that has done it and is a business success.

Foreword

Walt is not some slick salesman. He won't tell you what you want to hear. He tells it like it is and doesn't sugarcoat his message. You'll learn from him.

'Building Business 4 Success' gives you the strategies, opportunities and pitfalls of having your own enterprise. After reading the first 2 chapters, you will know for sure whether being in business for yourself is for you.

Many businesses fail due to poor planning and/or poor management. You can use 'Building Businesses 4 Success as a guidebook to be sure you have everything set up correctly and that you see and plan for the future. **It truly is a perfect blueprint for success.**

You may be a person with a skill, technology or idea that you want to launch into a business, but may know little about entrepreneurship. You'll learn about setting up a business. You'll also learn about sales, marketing, legal considerations and dealing with investors and the banks, etc.

After being in business for myself for over 30 years, I can honestly say that being an entrepreneur is an adventure that is not for everyone. It can be a roller coaster with the highest of highs and the lowest of lows. There is little more stressful and almost nothing more rewarding. You'll learn a lot about yourself and you'll get great at solving challenges and dealing with people. It will be one of the most exhilarating experiences of your life! Reading Walt's book will prepare you for this ride.

Foreword

~ Jordan Adler, investor, friend, author

Walt Camping, April Longa, Granddaughter

INTRODUCTION

Walt Camping

All of us, at one time or another, have dreamed about owning and running our own business. This is probably the second strongest part of the American dream we are taught, next to home ownership. We work for someone else and see how our efforts are helping them achieve their dreams. At some point we ask ourselves: why can we not do the same thing for ourselves? We have the technical knowledge and can talk to people and have some sales knowledge, so why not?

Introduction

For most, the answer is very clear: *"We're afraid to take a chance and risk failing!"*

So, we stay in our jobs. We build a lifestyle we're comfortable with. When we think about starting our own business, we're just dreaming of what might have been.

There is a saying that:

> *Some people make things happen*
> *Some people watch things happen, and*
> *Some people wonder what happened...*

<u>Which are you, but more importantly,</u> **which do you want to be?**

When presented with that question, most people will immediately answer that they want to make things happen. **Unfortunately, too few of us ever take the steps and risk needed to make it happen.**

Since you're reading this book, I'll assume that you do want to make it happen. You want to become an entrepreneur and leave behind the job you once knew. You want to create a life that allows you to live out your dreams instead of just working for someone else. Or maybe you're still on the fence and haven't decided to start your own business yet. In either case the first question you need to answer is:

Can you be your own businessman/businesswoman?

The answer to that question is:
OF COURSE YOU CAN!

Anyone can start a business, and anyone can succeed in business. So yes, you can be your own businessman. By simply having the desire, and the inclination to do so, you can start a business. It's not just the

Introduction

question of **can you** that matters though. That is the first question. There are other questions which need to be answered.

Appearances can be deceiving, and you need to consider a myriad of things other than your technical competency in the field you are accomplished in.

Maybe you're a wonderful plumber, accountant, landscaper, salesman, teacher, Internet online marketer, or whatever vocation your experience that has made you accomplished. But, do you have what to it takes to succeed in your own business?

Being in business for yourself not only has its benefits, but also its drawbacks and problems. So, why do you want to go into your own business? Here are some of the most common reasons.

- For the income and benefits?
- For the security and future of your family
- To control your own personal time management and schedule
- To be your own boss
- To prove something to yourself and/or others
- To help others
- It is your dream
- You want freedom to control your destiny

I am sure your reasons are all or part of the above and possibly even more. With the knowledge that you can go into business, and a basic understanding of why you want to, it's time to give you the other skills you need to find success.

Over the course of this book I hope to educate and prepare you for the wonderful opportunity of being a business owner/entrepreneur. More importantly I will give you the tools you need to minimize the problems and drawbacks you may encounter. <u>I can surely tell you that they will be there</u>, <u>but nothing that we cannot deal with</u>.

Introduction

The rewards **FAR OUTWEIGH** the problems that may come. And the greatest thing that you need to do for yourself is to **START YOUR BUSINESS!**

In other words, get off your couch and start doing what I will teach you. **Nothing is so damaging to your future as to do nothing, TO NOT ACT!**

A great friend and mentor of mine told me once that:

"If it is worth doing, it is worth doing poorly the first time"

In other words, **Don't worry about getting everything in place and right the first time; solving all the problems, making sure you know everything before you start your business, Just START IT** and the rest will fall into place. **We will handle these situations and problems as they come.**

With my training and help, you will handle whatever comes to you.

There is much that you need to know to be successful and secure. I will give you everything you need to become a success in your business. But, before we start on this wonderful journey together, let's begin with a little background and history of myself.

Background – So Who Am I To Teach YOU About Business?

I was born in Denver Colorado in 1943 to a father and mother who were Bakers in the family business. They had just gone through the Depression and World War II was going full force. My father had stopped school in the 8th grade to help in the family bakery business.

My parents were taught a work ethic and respect for their fellow man and their customers. They were also taught the understanding that the customer is the most important part of any business, **for if there**

Introduction

is not a sale, there is not a business. These were also taught to me as I grew up.

During high school, my brother and I got up at 4 AM each school day and helped my father in the bakery before going to school. We always complained about it, but later in life we grew to appreciate what Dad had done for us. I learned to be a self-starter and to see a task through to its conclusion.

I graduated from High School in 1962 and went into the US Navy and served 4 ½ years at the beginning of the Vietnam conflict. I loved flying and airplanes, so I was educated in Air Traffic Control (ATC) Naval Schools and did so on Midway Island and Point Mugu Naval Air Station in California before I was honorably discharged in August of 1966. I then joined the Phoenix Police Department where I served until December 1971. During my time as a police officer, I went to college and earned my Associates of Arts (AA) degree. In 1972 I resigned from the police department and started selling automobiles for the largest Chevrolet dealer in Arizona. I did this for 3 years until the first gas crisis hit our country.

Having a wife and 5 children, and car sales severely compromised by the gas shortage, I found a job selling lawn sprinkler systems with the oldest and largest company in Arizona. I worked my way up in the company to General Manager (GM) over the next 4 years when in 1978, I had the opportunity to start my own business.

I think it is important to stress to you that I never went a day in my adult life without a job. It was my responsibility to provide for the family, so I did what I had to, to accomplish this goal.

On a personal note: Do not let anyone tell you that you cannot get a job or that there are no good jobs for you. YOU have control of your destiny and future, and can do anything you set your mind to,

Introduction

IF YOU WANT TO! You only have to believe in yourself, and then GO DO IT!

Now remember that I had a wife and 5 children ranging in ages from 4 to 12. I think it is obvious to you that we did not have very much, but enough to take care of the family and send our children to a private school. So the chance I was taking was, to say the least, more scary and uncertain for my wife and family, than for me.

As a matter of fact, I had to borrow $8000 from the bank to start my business. I believed in the company (ServiceMaster) I got a franchise from, but more importantly **I believed in MYSELF**.

This company was the largest residential and commercial cleaning company in the world and had developed training and business procedures that, if learned and followed, would make one successful. We did just that, and in 5 years we built the largest residential franchise in the history of the company to that date in Phoenix, Arizona.

In 1987, ServiceMaster bought my businesses and I remained as a consultant for 2 more years. I received a check for $345,000 dollars for that sale. I set aside $95,000 for taxes, and invested the rest in real estate.

Now most of you may not remember what happened in the late 80's in real estate in this country, but this period was when the S&L (Savings and Loan) scandals occurred in the United States. Suffice it to say in 1989 land and property values in the country plummeted to less than 40% of their 1987 values were. Many residential and Commercial properties were lost because they could not be cash flowed to meet loans and mortgages. (sounds familiar today). All of my properties were affected and we lost them all. We were at a point that we had to start over.

Along with my 2 oldest boys, I was now looking for a business to start

Introduction

with them. We discussed the options and started a repossession business in Phoenix, Arizona. (www.campingcompanies.com) We only intended to build the business to a place where it would comfortably take care of our families. But, over the course of 11 years the business grew to 9 branches in 3 states.

By 2000, it became clear to us that managing the business was a very expensive and time-consuming operation. If we wanted to know how a branch operation was doing, we physically had to go to that location. So, after discussing the options, we made the decision to develop software to help in the management and growth of the company. The software was developed and went operational in 2002 and has been upgraded and refined since, to the point that it is now being sold to the industry nationally. (www.re-pros.com) Since 2000 we have added 6 more branch offices and are now the largest company in our industry nationwide.

I hope you can see, my background and experience has been varied and extensive in the business world. And I hope this gives you confidence that what I will try and teach you in this book will be accurate, correct and **WILL WORK** to make you successful, *if you follow it*.

As you can see, I have developed into a "Jack of ALL Trades and a Master of None." It has served me well and I hope you too will see the great advantage and ability in knowing **a little about many different things.**

Starting your business will require that you **take a RISK** and step out to grab your future for yourself and your family. I have made many mistakes and failures, **but I never gave up**, and if one door closed for me, I turned and went another way. And I had a lot of fun building my businesses along the way, as I am sure you will also, and you need to always keep that in mind.

The important thing for you to realize is that the joy you get and give

Introduction

in your life comes **as you travel down life's road, <u>not when you get to the end.</u> THE JOURNEY IS MUCH MORE IMPORTANT THAN THE DESTINATION!**

Remember that you came into this world with nothing and you will surely leave it the same way. There is no U-haul truck behind the hearse. It is only important what you do with what you are given that will give you satisfaction and joy, for your business, you life, your family and yourself.

The first half or our lives we strive for **SUCCESS**, and the last half of our life we strive for **SIGNIFICANCE.**

Our 16 Grandkids

Enough about me, except to say that I hope your confidence in myself and my abilities to help you has been strengthened. I also wish you all of the best in your own endeavors as we begin a journey that will help you on the road to business success. Without further ado, let's just dive right in.

CHAPTER 1 - WHY DO BUSINESSES FAIL?

I am sure many different feelings come over you, as you decide to start your own business. Excitement, fear, trepidation, joy, anticipation, sweating, clammy hands, uncertainty, and many other emotions may have been running through your head. For that reason, I think it would be important to give you a little information on why new businesses fail. The reasons are actually many, but I will list the main ones here.

My intention here isn't to discourage you or to start on a negative note. I simply want to start with failure because it's important to know why most businesses fail, **so that you don't**. These simple tidbits of knowledge will help to ensure that you don't end up falling flat on your face before your business even gets off the ground.

I will cover each of the reasons in more detail as we go along, but let's just start with a list. There are 8 reasons that are the most common causes of startup business failures.

The list looks something like this:

1. You started your business for the wrong reasons
2. Poor Management
3. Fear of Failure - Lack of Self Confidence
4. Lack of Capital
5. Location, Location, Location
6. Lack of Planning
7. No Web Site
8. Expanding and Growing too fast

Let's cover each idea in a little more detail. Having a good general knowledge of common reasons for failure will help ensure that you don't follow suit as you start your business.

1) You started your business for the wrong reasons

If your reasons for going into business include: to be your own boss and not answer to anyone else, make a lot of money, or have more time - you would be totally wrong. In fact, if your only reasons for starting a business include those I just listed, you're almost doomed to failure right from the start. There has to be much more if you want to find real success.

First, you need to **have a passion** for what you do. Starting your own business often entails long hours. You'll be forced to put in time overcoming problems, working to grow your business, and in general you should plan to dedicate a large amount of time to your business. If you aren't passionate about what you're doing, right from the start, then I promise you that you'll give up before you get anywhere and fail.

There is a saying that **"A lot of people like what they do, but very few people do what they like."** When it comes to going into business for yourself, if you don't like what you're doing, then you won't find the drive to make it through as you grow your business.

Next, **your service/product must fill a need to your customer.** Too many people start a business with the dream of making a pile of money, but along the way they forgot to find out if the business/product they are starting actually matters to someone else. If you don't have customers, you won't make money, period!

Most importantly **you need to have PMA (Positive Mental Attitude)**. No matter what happens, you need to get up and keep on going. **Don't be afraid to fail,** we all fail at some point or another. Remember, "It is better to have tried and failed, than to never have tried at all".

You also need to **have high integrity and character**, for if you do not, it will destroy you, your life and your business.

What it really comes down to is that you need to start your business for the right reasons. You need to **be passionate** about what you're about to do. You need to **be filling a need** in your market, and you need to **be willing to stick with it no matter what**. If you don't have at least one reason on your list that will help you find the drive and determination needed to succeed, then you most likely won't.

2) Poor Management

Many people think that if they know the technical part of the business that is all that's needed. But the lack of business knowledge in money and finance, sales and marketing, inventory Management, etc. show a neglect of the business.

You must always continue to learn all you can about planning for and working towards success. And, you must not be afraid to ask for help and counsel. You need to learn to be a manager that is a leader, has people skills, can delegate, has vision, is a risk taker, and is not afraid of change. This may seem like a tremendous challenge, but don't let it stop you in your pursuit of success! If you don't have all these qualities, find someone who has them to help you grow.

3) Fear of Failure - Lack of Self Confidence

This is probably the number 1 reason that new startups fail. Looking at the statistics: 68% of businesses never make it past the 2nd year, 50% never make it past the 4th year, and only 25% of the remaining businesses will be really successful beyond the 4th year (because they have done what I am going to teach you). **Fear of failure is the number one reason that the majority of businesses won't be around past year 2.**

No matter how much Technical, Sales and Marketing, Management or Financial expertise you may have, unless you are <u>**WILLING TO TAKE A RISK AND FAIL**</u>, you will never succeed in your own business.

As I have already said, you have to get out of your comfort level and take chances. If you take a look at many of the 20th and 21st century millionaires, you will find that they failed many times.

Did you know that Babe Ruth struck out over 2000 times. But, what do we remember him for?

Not his strikeouts, but the home runs he made.

Did you know that Thomas Edison failed over 1000 times in an attempt to discover the light bulb?

But he said, "I did not fail 1000 times, but found 1000 ways that did not work."

So, when you fail, and we all will and do, look at it as a learning experience, not a failure. For it is by these experiences that we grow and build confidence in ourselves and our ability to do whatever we want.

4) Lack of Capital

People who quit their day job to start a business think that they'll be able to have much more time to do what they want, but instead they sit around in their underwear watching soap operas and daytime talk shows and get just as little work done as they would have otherwise. They are not motivated to get cash into the business. Well, let me tell you,

CASH WILL DICTATE JUST HOW MOTIVATED YOU ARE OR HAVE TO BE!

Even if you're convinced that you're not like them, that you'll be super motivated, that you'll actually *enjoy* banging your head against the wall, and that by quitting your job you'll have infinite time, there's the constraint of money. It takes money to try different ideas, and when you're not working, that's usually in very limited supply. Remember, expenses occur every month, but profits may not quite cover them and, unless you sell something and bring in cash, you won't know when the profits will.

That is why you need to grow your business as fast as possible, based on available cash resources, so that sales overcome expenses quickly. When that happens, you have reached what is known as "Breakeven Point". In order to know what cash you will need, you need to **plan your work, and then work your plan.** My system will teach you this so you can plan you financial needs.

One thing I would like to say at this point concerning money is that although it is extremely critical to your business, it can be offset by one thing and that is **SALES AND MARKETING!** I should also note that a brick and Mortar type company will require more money than an E-commerce or Online business.

5) Location, Location, Location

If you are running a retail, service, or any other business that requires a physical plant or store, this is extremely important. You have to do your homework to determine where the right location is for you. Some of the things you should consider are:

1. Who and where are your customers
2. Where will you get the best traffic for your business
3. Where is your competition
4. Can you get any local government assistance for your start up business

5. Does the physical location you are considering work well for your business
6. Does the area need your type of business
7. Can you afford the monthly dollar expense for the location

If you are running an E-commerce or online business, this issue will not exist initially, but may come into play later in your business life as you grow and hire employees. The time will be determined by your growth, and I can tell you that when the time comes you will know it.

6) Lack of Planning

When you went camping, you did some planning. When you played a sport, you planned a strategy. When you took a trip, you planned your route and itinerary. You all have planned much more than you think; you just may not have known it. There are activities in our lives that require planning, and it is no different in business.

In your business the tool that we will use is called a Business Plan or Executive Summary. As you start the business, this plan will be very simple and easy. But as you grow, the plan will change and grow with you and will get more complicated. But I cannot over emphasize that you <u>**ALWAYS**</u> use the **KISS (Keep It Simple Stupid) Principle**.

Your Business Plan must always be flexible and fluent. It can never be cast in stone or you will suffer irreparable damage. <u>**This document is used for internal purposes only and should never be given to the outside world.**</u>

Your Business Plan should contain information on Sales, Marketing, Financial, Accounting, Employees and Human Relations, Capital,

Advertising, Budgeting and many other areas. We are developing financial tools to assist you in building your business, and as these become available we will put them on our website for you. We are also working on several planning tools for you. These will also be made available to you on our website.

7) You must have a website

If you want your business to be successful, it is **IMPERATIVE** that you have a website and Internet presence. Over 88% of the population were users of the Internet in 2008, and today that figure approaches 96%.

In 2007, non-travel-related e-commerce sales reached $175 billion, a 21% increase over the previous year, according to Forrester Research Inc. In its report, titled "U.S. E-Commerce Forecast: 2008 to 2012," Forrester predicts that online retail sales will reach $204 billion in 2008, $235.4 billion in 2009, $267.8 billion in 2010, $301 billion in 2011, and $334.7 billion in 2012. Actual Reported by the Centre for Retail Research, E-commerce is the fastest growing retail market in **Europe**. Sales in the **UK, Germany, France, Sweden, The Netherlands, Italy, Poland and Spain** are expected to grow from £132.05 bn [€156.28 bn] in 2014 to £156.67 bn [(€185.39 bn] in 2015 (+18.4%), reaching £185.44 bn (€219.44 bn) in 2016. In 2015, overall online sales are expected to grow by 18.4% (same as 2014), but 13.8% in the U.S. on a much larger total.

These figures relate only to **retail spending**, defined as sales of merchandise to the final consumer.

In the **US**, online sales are expected to rise from $306.85 bn [£189.26] in 2014 to $349.20 bn [£215.39 bn] in 2015 and $398.78 bn [£245.96 bn] a year later. **Canada**'s online sector is comparatively small, but is forecast to grow from US$20.82 bn [£12.84 bn] in 2014, to reach $23.56 bn [£14.53 bn] in 2015 and $26.99 bn [£16.65 bn] in 2016.

So as you can see, this one reason alone can cause you to drastically fail in your business endeavor. I will show you how to develop a website and host to post it for best coverage of your business on the web later in the book. Having a website in todays' business climate is **absolutely essential!!!!!!**

Even if you just run a service business, and you don't actually sell anything online - In our increasingly connected world, the web is how people find products and services. It is no longer enough to put an ad in the phone book. The Internet is the important, no imperative part of any marketing plan today.

8) Expanding your business too fast

When you start your business it is a common misconception that the faster you grow your business the quicker and more successful it will be. "If $5000 a month in sales is good, $25,000 a month in sales will be 5 times better." **THIS IS GROSSLY FALSE.**

When sales go up, so do expenses and cash flow is affected. I will explain more to you about this misconception in a latter chapter. Suffice it to say, you **must** grow your business, because a stagnate business will fail and die. But, **you must grow your business logically with an overall plan.**

With some of the main reasons that businesses fail out of the way, it's time to move on to bigger and better things. In the next chapter we'll introduce to you the 12 Hats of business. The Hat you wear could affect your success or failure, but as you'll see as we move through the rest of this book – **it's all about the Hats!**

YOU HAVE TO JUGGLE MANY BALLS (HATS) AT ONE TIME!

CHAPTER 2 - IT'S ALL ABOUT THE HATS YOU WEAR

We have explained to you the major reasons that your business may fail, and it is now time to look at the Hats you'll need to wear to make you a great success in business. As a business owner you'll need to wear many different Hats, sometimes in the same day, to find success. Really, you're about to learn that it's all about the Hats! And when we are done teaching you these Hats, I want you to be a **"Jack of all Trades (Hats) and a Master of none."** *I want you to know a little about each Hat, but not a lot about only one Hat.* This is the major trait of an Entrepreneur and successful businessman.

Of course in this case I'm not talking about the latest fashion hat from

Macy's. What I am referring to as a Hat is one area in your business that you must have knowledge of.

As I stated earlier to you, knowing the technical side of your business (doing the job) is a foregone conclusion. Other factors/Hats will become very important to you as you build your business. You either have to have knowledge in these areas or have someone in your business that does.

Being able to switch Hats as needed is important to finding success. One single area of knowledge (Hat) will never be enough to take you to financial security, and by learning how to wear all of the 12 Hats I'm about to introduce, you'll be doing a huge part in working towards your own future as an entrepreneur.

It's important to remember that even as you're starting your business, you aren't necessarily alone. Who are some of the people that can help you to get started and fill some of those Hats, and help you produce sales?

- Friends
- Relatives
- Business Associates/Organizations
- Professional Acquaintances
- People you do business with

These are just a few of the contacts you have to help you get started. When I started my ServiceMaster carpet cleaning business, I could not get extensive training for 2 months, so with the limited training and knowledge I did have, I contacted people from the list above and did over $4,000 in sales the first month. Remember, this was in 1978.

What is important in this example is not the amount of sales, but the fact that there <u>were sales</u>. Remember what I said earlier? <u>"Without Sales, Nothing Happens."</u>

Understand that some Hats will be needed sooner than others, but eventually, all will have to be a part of your business. There are 12 Hats that I refer to as the "Hats of Business" or the "Hats of the Businessman." Each one refers to a single area of knowledge, or a single skill set, that you will need. As I've already said some will be needed sooner than others, and sometimes you'll need one Hat more often, but all of them are important.

The 12 Hats of Business

To get you started, let's just cover what areas you're going to need knowledge and expertise in as you make your way to entrepreneurial success. Here are the 12 Hats I was referring to in the introduction to this chapter:

- Job Knowledge/Technical
- Business Management/Administration
- Technical/Computers
- Planning - Short and Long Term
- Sales and Marketing
- Customer Service, Customer Service, Customer Service
- Accounting and Finance
- Legal and Corporate
- Banking and Working Capital

- **Retirement and Estate Planning**
- **Continuing Education**
- **Know your Competition**

These Hats, as I like to call them, will make all the difference in you being a success or a failure in your business. Throughout the rest of this book I will be covering what each Hat is, and give you the information you will need to wear each Hat.

So, let's look at each, and by the time we're done talking about Hats (you don't have to call them Hats, you could call them shoes to fill if you want) we'll bring it all together so that you can see how each Hat fits into the picture of YOUR successful business.

CHAPTER 3 - THE HAT OF KNOWLEDGE

The first Hat we need to cover is the Hat of knowledge. In this case we're talking about knowledge of the main job role in the business that you are starting.

WALT CAMPING

For most, this is by far the easiest Hat for you to wear, because it is the reason you even thought about going into business in the first place. But it is no less important than any of the other Hats.

You must remember though that you have spent years learning your trade/job/expertise and will be the most comfortable in this area for that reason. Notwithstanding this, you still need to continue to:

- Remain on top of continuing advances in technology in your trade/industry
- Keep current in licensing requirements for your trade/Industry
- Continue to learn how to do your job better and better.
- Find other employees that are knowledgeable in your trade/industry, and make sure you have continuing education and training for them.
- If continuing education is available to you, please make sure you take advantage of it.

Let me tell you my experience in this area.

When I started my ServiceMaster Franchise in 1978, I knew nothing about how to clean carpet, tile, furniture or anything else. Service-Master had an extensive training program and it became clear to me instantly that all I had to do was follow their training and I would be successful. Unlike most of you, I had no training in this business, so I followed the companies program and was very successful.

. . .

Another example that was totally opposite of that business was my next business that my sons and I started in 1988. After ServiceMaster bought me out in 1987, I stayed on for 2 years consulting, and in late 1988 started Camping Companies, Inc. – a repossession company in Phoenix.

I also had no experience in this industry and there was no training available anywhere, so we learned over several years through the "School of Hard Knocks," with two totally different businesses that I made extremely successful. Why? Because I always looked to learn all I could about the business so I could be ahead of my competition, and I BELIEVED IN MYSELF!

There is not too much more to say except that you need to be aware of what's changing in your trade/industry at all times. Be out there looking, learning, teaching, doing, talking about what has made you so excited about your future, and what you can do to make your business more efficient and profitable.

Some of this will come from prior job knowledge and some from experience when you're working in your business. Even with that said though, staying on top of your field will ensure you can keep your business on top as well.

If you're in the donut business then you better learn everything you can about donuts (and no, eating etiquette doesn't count). Even if you've spent the past 15 years baking donuts, that doesn't mean you won't need to stay on top of things. New toppings, new baking equipment, or better coffees may all be something your competition has. Wearing the Hat of knowledge, and continuing to learn about the industry, will help you keep your business ahead of the shop down the street.

This Hat becomes even more important if you're starting a business in an industry that you've never worked in before. If your business is shipbuilding and you've never even been on a boat, then you have some work ahead of you. Knowing everything you can about your industry ahead of time will give you the knowledge you need to get your business off the ground.

Along with ensuring that you are current in the industry, wearing the Hat of knowledge also means being able to give your employees everything they need to help you stay ahead.

Most industries have tools like trade magazines, trade shows specific to the industry, and many even have training programs for them and their employees. Investing in these types of tools will help you to stay ahead in the long run.

CHAPTER 4 - THE MANAGEMENT & ADMINISTRATION HAT

The next Hat we want to cover is the manager's Hat. Now this particular Hat could feasibly include every other topic we cover in this Book. We could talk about the manager as the salesman, the manager as the accountant, etc. As a manager you need more knowledge of the business than any other employee, and you need to be able to deal with many different areas of the business. What I want to cover now is the manager as the administrator.

As you start your business, this Hat will require less of your time, but as your company grows, it will become increasingly more important, as will all the Hats, and must be dealt with regularly and with flexibility.

However, there are some things you will have to do initially that will require some time and money, but are essential to you and your business. In this chapter we will cover the administrative tasks that you'll need to perform now, and we'll talk about some that you should expect in the future.

Your First Ten Administration Tasks

Especially when you are just starting out, there are some administrative tasks that you need to take care of immediately. Most of these are simply ensuring you have the right elements in place to setup and start your business (i.e. a business name).

Here are the ten things you need to do now:

- One of the first things you need to do as a manager is to **obtain a name for your business and form an entity** within the state you reside in.

    The entity will be one of the following:
    -Sole proprietorship (SP)
    -Partnership (PS)
    -Limited Liability Corporation (LLC)
    -S Corporation (SC)
    -C Corporation (CC)

Each of these has both positive and negative features. I suggest that you consult with an attorney for assistance, but, in my past experience, let me say that you should initially look at forming your company as an LLC or SC. This will give you legal benefits of varied degrees to protect you and insulate you as an individual, and your company.

There are also tax benefits of each and your accountant can explain them to you. An LLC gives you more protection or tax benefits comparatively than an SP, and A CC is something you may consider as the business grows, but you will need counsel from both your Attorney and Accountant.

If you setup an LLC, SC or CC, you may have to set up Corporate Books, issue Stock and create Articles of Incorporation and Bylaws. Most of this will be part of the process that you will do setting up the corporate entity, but you still need to know that these need to be accomplished as part of that process.

There are two ways to start your company. You can do it the more traditional way and seek out the help of an attorney (you'll need an attorney anyway), or in our age of ever-increasing Internet connectivity you can also use sites like http://www.llc.com/ or www.legalforms.com to start your LCC company online. In either case I do suggest you talk to your attorney to find out which type of company is best for you.

- **Find an Attorney and an Accountant** that you can have available if and when you need them to consultation. Don't put them on retainer!

- **Register the name of your business** with the Corporation Commission or entity that governs companies in your state.

- If you are a retail business, you will have to **apply for sales tax licenses** in your local, county and state agencies.

- You will also have to **obtain a business license** from all the cities/localities you do business in. In some areas you may have to obtain a license only in the city you have you business in, but check local requirements to see what you will have to do.

- **Obtain a Domain Name** for your business. This can be done very easily by going to Google and entering "Domain Names" on your computer. This will give you several sites you can go to. I have used Godaddy.com, Register.com, and Networksolutions.com.

Whoever you use, make sure you protect your business name. The reason for this is that once you have the domain name for you business, you can create a website and email addresses that associate with the business. All advertising materials and correspondence will tie to it. This one step is one of the most important things you can do for your new business!!!

- **Obtain a Federal Employee Identification Number (EIN)** for your business. This Number will be the basis of all identification to the financial and investment community in the business world. Go to www.irs.gov/businesses/small/article/0,,id=102767,00.html

- Set up a **Business Checking account**

- **Setup an accounting system** for your business. I would suggest you purchase QuickBooks for Business. www.**QuickBooks**.com. It is inexpensive, complete and capable of handling small and medium sized businesses.

- **Design and get Business cards**, stationary, etc for your company. I recommend Vistprint.com for this.

- **Trademark/Register your logo/Company Motto.** This can be done when you register your name with the corporation commission.

Management and Administration as You Grow

Now that we have done the logistically small but important initial things to get your business up and operating, it now is important that you understand what you will have to do in the future, as your business grows, in the management and administration area.

You'll likely find that as you grow you take on less of the daily technical and operational tasks (you'll have others to do that for you), but management and administration go hand in hand and they will always be important. Without ensuring you are on target, or without having a clear idea of where you are now or where you are going, you'll eventually find your business will become stagnate and growth will stop and your business will fail.

The actual management aspects of your business will be specific to your industry. But I do want to give you some ideas of what you'll need to face as you grow.

As you grow, you must always be looking at how your business will be perceived by the world. Here are a few examples of things that can go wrong if you do not keep control of the growth of the company and manage it effectively:

1. If you have **no clear strategy**, you will continually reorganize in ways that impeded, rather than encourage strategic success, and you will fail.
2. If the company is **lagging visibly behind in a fastest-moving industry**, you must concentrate on current successful strategies to will make your business successful.
3. **Do not get bogged down by overlapping services and operations**, indecision, or a top-heavy management structure. Keep it simple stupid **(The KISS principal).**
4. As a manager you need to work to grow your business, but *Do not try to grow too fast!*

5. **Keep all the cash you can** as you build your business. This is one of the most important management jobs you will have, for without CASH, you will fail. When I started my businesses, I was seriously undercapitalized, as most businesses are, but I had the ability to get sales and business loans and investors to help. However, in the business climate today, it will be much harder to find business capital and investors and will require you to become much more inventive, innovative and creative in your quest for capital.

With some of the ideas about administration out of the way it's time to move on. In the next chapter we're going to get a little more technical and talk about the age of computers, and your new technical hat!

CHAPTER 5 - THE TECHNICAL HAT

The next Hat you need to wear is the technical Hat. In this case I'm referring to computers. In an age where everything is tied to Computers, Social Media and Technology, to Twitter, Facebook, YouTube, etc. and the extensive use of the Internet for all areas of daily life, this Hat is one that you will have to be extremely versed and proficient in, and will be using on a daily basis.

I would say that virtually all of the different Hats of your business can and MUST be done by computers and programs you can run on them. Some examples are:

- Business Management – See the 10 items that I listed for you in the last chapter.
- Accounting- An Accounting Software to run the business
- Planning- Software programs for Inventory, Ordering, and Warehousing, if required.
- Sales and Marketing information, software, mailing lists, Customer Lists, CRM, etc.
- Use of Excel, Word and Power Point to create graphs and charts to show trends in growth, sales, vendors, planning, etc.
- Job Knowledge- you can stay on top of advances, innovations, training and certifications to keep you on top of and ahead of your competition in competency and knowledge.

When it comes to things like building websites and that type of technical knowledge you can always hire someone else to do it. But basic computer skills you are going to need to be proficient.

Let's face it, if you start your business without the use of computers, but your competitor down the street will be using them; thus they will have a distinct advantage over you from the get go. They have a better data set to work with to analyze and grow their business, they have better records for accounting, and in general they are probably more organized than you. Computer use for business isn't really an option anymore. You need, and will not be able to exist, without computers, and you need the knowledge to use them well.

. . .

Luckily in our connected world, getting these skills isn't difficult, and it doesn't have to cost a lot.

Here are some ways to take your technical knowledge further if you don't have the skills needed in this area.

1. **Take Free Courses Online** – If it's basic computer skills you need, you can visit sites like Home and Learn to get basic computing courses for free. I found this site by doing a simple search on Google.com, so if those courses don't suit, search again. There are dozens of sites with information like this for free.
2. **Read a Book** – There are literally hundreds of books out there that can give you a broader knowledge of computers, or that can teach you a very specific area of computer use. I particularly like the For Dummies Books series. Most of them are easy to read, and they include dozens of titles that work for business. Titles like Quickbooks 2018 for Dummies, Excel for Dummies, Microsoft Office for Dummies, and others may make getting those skills fun and easy.
3. **Take a more formal course** – You can also take courses to learn almost any aspect of computer use. You'll find online courses, and more formal classroom led courses if you prefer. These can be a great way to learn computer skills. If you are looking for courses on a specific piece of software, you should take the time to browse the software vendors site. For example Inuit leads many different types of QuickBooks Training. You can also find courses on Microsoft Office, Web Design, and pretty much any topic you can think of.

However you decide to gain the PC skills you need, keep in mind that you do need them. That $50 invested in books or $150 invested in online courses will take you a long way in ensuring you get your business started the right way.

In the next chapter we're going to put on our planning hat and have some fun. Planning is one of the most overlooked and underused aspects of starting and running a business, and for many it will mean the difference between success and failure.

CHAPTER 6 - THE PLANNER'S HAT

I am sure you have heard the saying to "plan your work and work your plan." As simple and elementary that this sounds, it is very true. And as your business grows, you will spend more and more time in the planning stages of the company.

Initially though, as you start your business, planning will be as simple as

- What do I do today?
- What materials do I need to get to finish this job?
- I have to make an invoice to give the client when I finish today.
- Do I need to pay some bills today?
- Do I have enough money to get some groceries today?
- What do I have to do to get more out of my day as it relates to priorities, etc, etc, etc.

Most of your planning will be done "On the Run, as situations dictate, on a daily, hourly or minute basis." I remember when I started my first business, the one glaring planning problem I had was "how was I going to make enough money to make ends meet this week." And I venture to say this will be your first planning problem also. I knew my trade, so I just focused all my energies on finding people who needed my Product/Service and getting the business.

I needed $4000 gross for the month to make my personal financial responsibilities. I broke it down to smaller pieces that I could handle better. I knew that to clean the carpet in an average home would be around $100. To clean an average chair was $40. So I took my monthly goal of $4000, divided it by 4.3 weeks in a month, which equaled $930 per week. I then divided this into 6 days a week I could do work. This equaled $155 per day.

Therefore, I now knew what my daily planning goals were, and I started out contacting friends, relatives and businesses I knew to get work. In my first month, with little training, I made $4150. I then did the same thing the next month and so on. And as sales grew, my planning became more detailed and long term, but I always did the fundamental planning regularly that I did when I started in business.

When I started my first business, which was a franchise, the first thing I was asked to do was to put down my 1, 3 and 5-year sales goals. Interesting enough, I had just done my first month of business of $4150, so I thought about it for a few days and then called my distributors and informed them I had my sales goals. Now understand that I had not even been trained completely and knew very little about the business. But:

I KNEW MYSELF AND WHAT I COULD DO AND BELIEVED IN MY TALENTS AND HAD CONFIDENCE IN MYSELF!

I told them I would do $100,000 in year 1, $500,000 in year 3, and $1,000,000 in year 5.

There was complete and total silence on the phone and I finally had to keep asking if my distributors were there. I did this for almost a minute until they finally answered me. I later found out that they were so shocked by my goals that one of them fell out of his chair and other just sat there in disbelief. They came back on the phone and said that my goals were "extremely ambitious and maybe unrealistic." They suggested I should revisit the goals and get back to them with more "Realistic Sales Goals." I was courteous and said I would, but told them a few days later that I was sticking with these goals.

Now understand that this was 1978, and the goals I had set for myself had never been contemplated before in the company. I made a graph

WALT CAMPING

that I put on the wall to remind me of what I had committed myself to. I then broke down the yearly goals into monthly, weekly and daily goals using financial formulas I will explain to you shortly. Needless to say, in my first year we did $108,000,

In our 3rd year we did $ 556,000, and in our 5th year we did $1,046,000. I cannot really tell you how we met these sales goals other than to say that if you commit your plans to writing and always keep them visible and viable, **you will make them.**

The tool we used in formulating our sales goals was a financial model called the "Rule of 78's." This was an interest tool used to finance vehicles back in the 70's and 80's but was later dropped from use as being grossly unfair and usurious. But for the purposes of sales goals planning, it was and still is a great tool when you are planning sales growth.

Let me give you an example of the Rule of 78's.

Let's go back to my 1-year sales goal of $100,000. Normally, you would divide this figure by 12 and get a figure of $8,333.34. This is an average for each month. However, when you start out a new business you will not immediately get to that average. You have to build up to it, hence the Rule of 78's.

Here how it works. If you take the 12 months of a year --- Month 1, Month 2, Month 3 and so on, and add all of the months,---1,2,3,4,5,6,7,8,9,10,11,12, the total is 78. So, using this basis, you would divide your yearly sales goal, in this case, $100,000 by 78, which equals $1282. So, this means that your sales will grow by $1282 per month as shown in the table below. To equal your yearly sales of $100,000.

Month 1	Month 2	Month 3
$1282	$2564	$3846
Month 4	Month 5	Month 6
$5128	$6410	$7692
Month 7	Month 8	Month 9
$8974	$10,256	$11,538
Month 10	Month 11	Month 12
$12,820	$14,100	$15,382

This formula is more logical and justified and does not put so much pressure on you as you plan sales goals each month and year. One other thing to consider in your planning using this tool is that if you have sales that are <u>recurring each month</u>, at the beginning of the 13th month of sales, you will already have sales of at least $15,382 x 12 months for the next year which equals $ 184,584 for year 2 before you even add new sales goals into the planning sequence. But if your sales are <u>new each month</u>, you can still use this formula in your planning. Either way, this formula is much more accurate, logical and fair in projecting **CONTROLLED** growth in your business.

You may have realized that the only planning we have discussed thus far has dealt with sales. I hope by now you understand why this is so extremely important and critical, because as I have tried to impress on you previously,

Sales are the backbone of any business. <u>Nothing happens until a sale occurs!</u>

All other planning will revolve around and be totally dependent upon the sales you produce in the company. As sales grow, so will your planning in all other areas.

That isn't to say that you shouldn't plan all aspects of your business. You should. In fact a formal business plan will help you greatly, **but only after the first year,** after you are established. The plan should be a guide to show you how to get to years 2,3,4,5 and beyond, and should include your Hats from every aspect of your business, and you should be able to adjust your plan as needed. The important thing to note here is that **your sales are the most important aspect of that plan.** The money coming in will affect every other aspect of your business.

For some examples of more formal business plans visit this site: http://www.bplans.com/. The site itself sells some planning software, but if you click on samples or articles it also includes a lot of free information and samples of how to write a business plan. You should take some time to expand your knowledge in this area as it is an important part of your business both now and as you grow.

CHAPTER 7 - THE SALESMAN'S HAT

After understanding the Planning process, the next Hat we need to cover is your sales Hat. <u>On a scale of 1 to 10 Sales and Marketing ranks as 100!</u>

It is by every stretch of the imagination the most important Hat you will ever wear in your business. It makes no difference how much experience that you may have in all the other Hats combined, they will not stack up to or have the importance that this Hat does.

The reason I can say this is because of my past experience in my businesses. As I told you earlier in my Bio, my background was Sales and Marketing, and that trait was a major reason we were successful in all of our business ventures. I spent my time outside the office and my wife spent her time working on the internal Hats—Organizational areas.

People have said that you are born with the traits to be a salesman/women. I believe that is true to a degree, but as you can see from a general list of traits listed below, some of you are born with some traits, but some can be learned. Some examples are:

- We all are salesmen/women to some degree in our daily lives, we just don't think of it as selling.
- When we have found a good price on something we bought and told a friend/neighbor and try and convince them to buy it.
- When we are trying to convince a friend about a point we are making in a conversation.
- When we have an excellent idea to help our company and we try and convince our boss.
- And the biggest one of all—when we asked our husband/wife to marry us. WOW!

The traits of a good salesman generally include most if not all of the following:

- Enjoys learning new things
- Enjoys a challenge
- Has fun solving problems
- Has a creative and flexible mind
- Enjoys meeting new people

- Sets goals
- Makes and keeps appointments
- Finds the good in the bad
- Keeps abreast of trends
- Is a hard worker
- Builds & maintains relationships
- Looks for opportunities wherever he or she goes
- Is organized and a good planner
- Is enthusiastic about whatever he or she is selling
- Is knowledgeable about the products he or she is selling
- Knows who the competition is and what they are doing
- Rolls with the punches
- Deals with criticism well
- Shows respect to all potential customers
- Knows that he or she is more than his or her job
- Participates in community activities and affairs
- Is self-reliant
- Faces obstacles head on
- Is responsible and does whatever it takes to be successful
- Enjoys a well balanced lifestyle

Although different, super salesmen/women also have certain traits in common. The most apparent is this—they are all men/women of spirit. They intensely want to make sales. They can get hot —literally. They are alive. When they talk to a prospective buyer he feels their enthusiasm and responds to it. They never give up as long as there's the ghost of a chance to make a sale. They aren't afraid to ask for the order. They aren't intimidated by the tough prospects that try to discourage them. They are the spark plug and mainspring. They are a perfect example of the super salesman just described. They are confident without being chesty. They're poised and sure without being overbearing. They are a lot of fun, but always are driving for the order. They are not afraid to call on new prospects—in fact that might well be the greatest single secret of their success. The lifeblood of a business is the NEW blood in the form of new customers. (Posted by Estella effects)

In a blog on BLACK IN BUSINESS on February 6, 2009 "what a great salesmen/women is" gives us a look at great sales people with different backgrounds and upbringings:

"I started my career as a salesman for Xerox. Over the years I have developed an affinity for sales people. Most of my close friends are in sales. There must be a certain personality that makes up a salesman. As I think about salesmen, I wonder, are great salesmen, natural or can salesmanship be taught and there for learned.

My former neighbor in Columbia, Maryland, Dan Alexander was an incredible salesman. Dan was tall, 6ft 3 inches, impeccably dressed, and full of energy and a love of people. Dan was a life of the party type. Loud, always talking, Dan knew how to make things happen. I lost touch with Dan for many years, but one day during a visit to the nations capitol, I was reading the Washington Post's style section. There was my man Dan, the number one salesman in the nation for Niemen Marcus department store. Dan sold over 2 million dollars of men suits and accessories in one year.

My friend, Richard Burns is a great salesman and shares a lot of Dan's personality, loud, always talking and life of the party. Richard is quick witted and recently was the top salesman in the nation for his medical software company.

Larry Hernandez is another great salesman. If you get in a conversation with Larry and do not know what to say, believe me, Larry will fill in the blanks, he loves to engage and can fill up a room with his energy. Larry was the diagnostics industries top salesman before going into management.

My brother, David Davinchi, is the top car salesman in New England. David is tall, never shuts up and loves people. When we were little kids, I was the quiet one.

Darryl Gresham, an international brother, from Pittsburgh, now living on a golf course in South Africa. Like Larry, Darryl is not tall, however he has the same traits as the other brothers, I referred to. He is loud, life of the party and can talk for days. I hired Darryl back in Buffalo and he quickly became a top salesman and now he is a General Manager.

All of these guys were also athletes and remain very competitive. These men are gregarious for sure. How about salesmen like me. Quiet, even shy, friends like Bill Minix, the late Tom Jackson. All of us have been very successful in sales but are not quintessential sales personalities.

Those of us that are not natural born salesmen, had to be taught how to sell. We then learned how to be successful in sales. Maybe we were natural but because we were quiet, maybe we listen better. **The better you listen the better you understand your customer.**

Can salesmanship be taught? Can you be shy and quiet and still be an effective salesman? What role does a sales manager play in the development of a sales talent? In the medical field many of the best sales representatives are women. Are women better in sales than men? What traits do top salesmen that you would do business with have?"

I can go on and on about what a salesman/woman needs to have to be successful, but suffice it to say that this Hat will always be at the forefront of the business, because remember: *"Nothing happens until there is a Sale!"*

Selling Anything – The Right Way

Because of the importance of this area of business, I wanted to go a little further. Especially if you've never worked in a sales capacity, the task of selling anything can seem daunting. I'm going to tell you that it doesn't have to be, and I'm going to show you a simple way to look at selling so that you won't find yourself with clammy hands and cold sweats the first time you are faced with selling your product or service.

Rather than looking at sales as selling. Take the point of view that you are working to build relationships. As I will show you in the next chapter, in a sense that is what you are doing anyway, but it can be learned now as a selling style.

If you've visited a car dealership at any time over the past 10 years, then you've likely experienced the style of selling I'm about to teach you. It is how most modern day sales people on car lots are taught to sell (if you happen to catch an old-school salesman on the lot, they likely had a much pushier sales style).

The sales style is called the Reverse Pyramid style of selling and it looks something like this:

```
      Meet and Greet

      Needs Assessment

      Feature Benefit
       Presentation

        Close the
          Sale
```

The tiers in the pyramid represent time frames. As you can see the largest tier is given to meeting the client, next we move into assessing what the client needs, and in the two smallest sections at the end we start presenting a solution and finally close the sale.

The reason this style of selling is so effective is because the focus isn't actually on selling anything. It's on getting to know the client and building a relationship with them. It's much easier to sell something to someone who knows something about you, and trusts you (to a certain degree) than it is to sell to someone who doesn't know you at all.

Let's walk through each step, so that you'll have an idea of what to do in each step of the selling process. It's important to note here that the amount of time spent selling will vary depending on what you have to sell. If you're selling a big ticket item, such as a car or a piece of real estate, the process can take hours. If you're selling something smaller it may take minutes. What matters is that you take the time to get to know something about the client and to establish common ground. Customers will remember this and they will come back to you because of it.

Meet and Greet

The first stage of the selling process is simply getting to know your customer. In the meet and greet section of our sales process we simply ask open ended questions and work to find common ground with the customer. Always begin the meet and greet with an introduction and a hand shake. Beyond that the process will depend a little on what you're selling, but your goal here is twofold:

1. You are working to get to know the customer. The more you know about them the easier it will be to logically walk into the next three steps.
2. You are working to find common ground with the customer. People relate better to someone who they have something in common with. This may be anything from having kids to enjoying fishing, but common ground does work to build trust.

This step of the process is basically just talking. Anyone can do it, and by spending more time here you'll find the next three steps go smoothly.

Needs Assessment

After you've gotten to know something about the client it's time to move into the needs assessment. This is the part of the process where we find out why the customer is visiting you (or why they called if it's a service business). Basically we want to find out what they want from you, and more than that we want to find out their key selling points or hot spots.

. . .

Again this part of the process is just asking questions. You might ask why they visited and then follow up with a, why is that important to you? Stick to open ended questions and always follow the first question up with a why is that important, or what do you feel that will do for you?

By gaining this information you are getting down to the real reasons why the client is after your product or service. You'll find that the deeper reasons for their visit often have little to do with the original reason they stated they were there.

For example if you were actually selling a car, their initial statement may have been that they want to buy that specific model they saw on TV, but by the time you have finished with this part of the process you'll know that safety, and reliability matter and that the actual reason they came is because their old car has cost them $1,000 in repairs in the past two months. Suddenly you have key points that matter to them and can use those to both lead them to the right product, and ultimately to point out all of the benefits that actually matter.

Feature Benefit Presentation

Once you've finished with the second step of the process it's time to start selling your product. In this step you simply present your solution, but you focus on the benefits. More specifically you focus on the benefits that matter to the customer.

In the last step you took the time to find the key points as to why the customer was seeking your product or service. Now you simply present the product, and make your focus on how the product will take care of those key points.

. . .

You present a feature, and then ask a closed ended question that end with wouldn't it, couldn't it, or shouldn't it. For example, if you were selling a computer and one of the needs that you gained from the last step was "fast enough to play the latest high-end video games", you might point out the feature and benefit:

"This PC has a Quad-Core 5.0 Ghz CPU which means it's fast enough to run multiple programs at once, and it won't have any problems dealing with the latest 3D shooter game. That would be great, wouldn't it?"

The point here isn't on how to sell a computer; it's that we finish pointing out a benefit by asking if that would help them. What you are essentially doing is getting the customer to agree with you after every point. If you get a customer to say "Yes" several times, they will have a hard time saying no when we get to the last step.

Close the Sale

In our last step we close the sale. If you took the right amount of time on the first three steps, this portion of the selling process is usually as simple as asking "Will you be paying cash or credit card today?" or "So this is the one you want then?"

At this point one of two things will happen. The customer will either answer you, and buy the product, or they'll say no and you can start asking questions to find the reasons why they are saying no. By this point in the selling process you have built enough of a relationship with the client that they usually will tell you why they aren't ready to buy now and you can begin overcoming their objections.

How to destroy your business in five easy steps

The reason for marketing is simple: to attract more people to your business. However, it can be expensive, and if not done properly, ineffective. This has made it a tricky issue for startup businesses with small budgets. To work, marketing campaigns must be carefully targeted at the desired audience meaning there are few generic 'must do's'. However, there are some marketing disasters that all businesses should definitely avoid.

Chris Cardell is one of the UK's leading experts on small business marketing. He has been featured extensively on national media including BBC, ITV and the national press. After a decade of working with and interviewing hundreds of UK businesses, Chris has outlined five of the fatal mistakes that business owners and managers make, which at best cost them a fortune in lost profits – and at worst can lead to business failure.

1 - Not communicating effectively with your existing customers

Your best immediate sources of additional profits and increased business are your existing customers. These are the people who you've already invested time, energy and money with to create a relationship. They know you, they trust you, hopefully they've enjoyed doing business with you. Because of this it is normally five to ten times easier to get an existing customer to buy from you again, than it is to get someone to buy from you for the first time.

If this is the case, why are so many businesses so ineffective at communicating with existing customers? Here is an example that we can all relate to. Think of all the ads in your local newspaper for restaurants. Imagine all the money the restaurant owners are spending on these ads. Now ask yourself this question: When did you last receive a letter or an email from a restaurant you've visited, asking you to come back, or offering you a free bottle of wine if you bring your family? What would happen if your local restaurant asked for your email or your address at the end of your meal so that they could keep you informed on special offers, incentives, or perhaps to enter you into a prize draw for a free meal. What would happen to the first restaurant in your area to apply this systematically for the months and years ahead?

Now apply this principle to your business. Here are some useful questions to ask yourself. How often do you communicate with your existing customers? What do you have to offer your existing customers? What are you not offering existing customers that you could be offering them? When did you last send a letter to your customers? When did you last email them? Did you measure the response? When did you last call them? What would happen if you doubled your contact with them this year? When you do communicate with them, what more could your be doing to clearly explain the specific benefits that they will experience?

I once had a client who generated £300,000 by sending a brochure to their clients once a year. I asked what would happen if they sent the brochure twice a year. The thought had never even crossed their mind. We did it (and a lot more) and it generated a fortune for my client.

This may sound ridiculously simple but it is not an unusual story. We are all so close to our businesses that it is often a challenge to step back and look at the obvious – the elusive obvious.

When I start working with a new client, I know without a doubt that they are sitting on a goldmine. This goldmine consists of the wealth that is hidden in their relationships with their current customers.

Here are some more useful questions to maximize your relationship with existing customers: How often do you communicate with your customers by direct mail? Do you test and measure the response? Do you spend at least 15 minutes each month thinking of an exclusive offer you can make to your existing customers? Do you say 'thank you' to your customers either by letter, by email or by telephone? Do you ask your customers for referrals? Did you know that there are at least 90 ways of getting referrals? If you have a limited service or product line – do you know of additional companies, products or services that your customers could benefit from?

There are hundreds of great marketing strategies for getting new customers (we'll deal with some of them in the rest of the article) But, before that, you need to nurture your relationships with your existing customers. It is the first key to the goldmine.

2 - Relying on just one or two main forms of marketing

If you are similar to most businesses, there are probably one or two main forms of marketing that you are currently using to grow your business. It many be advertising, or referrals, or direct mail, your website, emails, PR, telemarketing, strategic alliances etc.

If you want to grow your business exponentially, your goal should be to turn your business into a multi – level marketing machine, where you are combining several of these marketing approaches simultaneously.

What do you think happens to a business that over the space of a year goes from using one or two main marketing methods to ten? This is how you grow a business by 100-300%.

Now if it's that simple, why aren't more businesses doing it? There are two reasons. The first is they just don't know how. They haven't realized that you will never fulfill your business potential if you don't make marketing a top priority.

The second reason is fear. If someone were to suggest that you go out next week and implement ten new marketing strategies, you would be justifiably concerned that you could lose money if the strategies went wrong – and that even if they were a success, the business might not be able to cope with such rapid growth.

That's why the principle of 'testing and measuring' is possibly the most important marketing concept there is.

The principle of testing and measuring is simple. Every month you should test one or two or more new marketing methods on a small scale. This could be a new ad, a new direct mail campaign, some telemarketing, etc. By testing small and measuring the results you quickly identify what works and what doesn't. When you find something that works, you roll it out on a larger scale.

It sounds ridiculously simple doesn't it? Guess how many businesses apply such a process systematically. Less than 1 in 50. Shocking but true. So make testing a fundamental part of your approach and you'll already be way ahead of the competition.

By the way, before you do any of this, you need to be testing and measuring the marketing that you are already doing. This is where most businesses are losing a fortune. For example, you wouldn't believe the number of businesses who advertise but have never measured the results, so they never really know if their advertising is working.

If you do what I suggest – and each month discover just one new marketing approach that works for you, through good testing, then this time next year you'll have twelve new marketing strategies producing results for you. What difference will that make to the strength, stability and profitability of your business?

3 - Running ineffective advertising

Advertising can be a highly effective way to increase your customer and client base…when it's done well. But, for many businesses advertising is ineffective because it's either not well written, or you haven't tested how well it's working, or you haven't experimented with different types of ads.

So here are some of the fundamentals of successful advertising:

First, it is absolutely essential that you test and measure the response to all of your advertising. So many businesses just allocate a certain mount of money to an advertising budget, spend the money every year - and they've only got a vague sense of whether the ads are working are not. This is crazy. If your ads are working, you want to roll them out on a larger scale. If they're not, change the ads or use the money on one of the dozens of other marketing strategies that can bring you a 100 or 200 or 300% return on your investments.

Unless you're a global multi national engaging in brand advertising, the purpose of your ads is to produce a response. You need to be able to measure that response, otherwise you're not going to know if the advertising is working. How many people responded, how many of them were converted to a sale, what's that worth to you? Compare that to the cost of the ad and you can immediately work out how profitable the ad was.

If this sounds obvious, it is but you would be amazed at how you can improve the response to your advertising with some simple testing and simple changes.

Here are some other fundamentals of advertising:

In the ad itself, the most important element is the headline. The headline is either the heading that goes at the top of the ad or if there's no heading it's the first words of the ad. The headline needs to grab peoples' attention. One change in a headline can produce a 50-100% increase in response.

The copy of your ad needs to be a personal communication to the individual reading it. And it needs to be about them. It needs to address their needs, desires and fears and it needs to constantly communicate the benefits of what you are offering. At the end of the ad you need a call to action. Tell people exactly what they need to do to follow through and make it easy for them to do so.

If you've got an ad that's working for you, it's worth testing some changes to the headline or the main copy to see what results it produces. Above all, step into the shoes of your potential customers while reading your ad to get a real sense of the impact that it will have. Which brings us to …….

4 – Failing to focus on the benefits that your product or service offers your customers and clients

If you go to buy a hi-fi, what are you actually buying? Are you buying the equipment – the combination of electronics and wires and the casing that surrounds it? Or are you actually buying the BENEFITS of the hi fi – the sound you will hear, the pleasure that sound will give you, perhaps the significance and joy that you get from owning a hi-fi larger than the guy down the street!

If you can accept and understand the following principle, your marketing will instantly improve. 'People don't buy your product or service. They buy the benefits that your product or service offers them.'

Understanding this simple distinction can transform your marketing. How? Because you will approach all of your marketing in a totally different way. Next time that you write a letter or brochure, or create a website or send an email or speak to a customer on the phone, every word will be crafted to ensure that your customer understand the benefits of what you have to offer.

Of course, this pre-supposes that you and your colleagues understand the benefits yourselves. This is not always as simple as it sounds. When we own or run a business, we are so close to what we do that we often lose sight of what it's like for our customers. Also, an important benefit for one customer might not be so important for another. You might choose a new car because of its speed and acceleration. Your neighbor may choose the same car because of its safety.

So spend some time getting clear on what exactly your benefits are – and then make sure that you articulate them precisely in all of your communications.

You can also turn this concept on its head and look at it another way. When people don't buy from you, one of the prime reasons will be because they don't understand and appreciate the full benefits of doing so. You can increase the percentage of people who buy from you by 20-40% just by focusing on getting them to understand precisely how they will benefit from doing business with you.

5 - Not using Email Marketing effectively

Let's step back a decade. Imagine if ten years ago, someone had told you that in the future you would be able to communicate directly to your customers or potential customers, sending them any message you chose and that it was absolutely free. No paper required, no printing, no envelopes, no brochures, no stamps. In addition, that message could be sent to anyone anywhere in the world. And as an added bonus, instead of having to wait 24 or 48 hours, it would arrive with them within seconds.

It would have sounded too good to be true, right?

Welcome to the world of email and E-marketing. Too many business owners and managers still haven't appreciated the power of email and the internet. The dot com bust caused many to write off the profit potential of the internet – a big mistake. In addition, the irritation that many people choose to feel about the emails they receive fails to take into account that email has become an incredibly important form of business communication.

To the extent that you are able to build E-marketing into your marketing mix, you will see an immediate return in both profits and enhanced customer relationships. The key is not to think of email as a selling tool – but as a powerful communication tool. Use it to give – to add real value to your customers' lives and to keep them informed on your activities. Here are some of the fundamental basics of E-marketing:

Capture everyone's Email address. You've heard this a thousand times before, but would you believe that most businesses still do not collect the email addresses of everyone who contacts them? You may as well take a huge bucket of cash, go to the top of your building and throw it out of the window. Every time a business fails to capture someone's email address they're turning down the opportunity to contact them for FREE, for weeks, months and years ahead. This is insanity. It's also insane not to offer visitors to your website an easy way of submitting their email address, so they can see if you are as good as you say you are. Your web designers should be able to set up a simple way of doing this. Once you have email addresses – use them! Of the businesses that are good at collecting email addresses, hardly any of them follow up by communicating regularly with their customers and clients in an effective way. You don't just have to use email to sell stuff. You can use email to thank people for their business, make them a special offer, give them a free article or report, send a newsletter, recommend a product or service they may be interested in, ask for referrals, share some news that may be interested in, ask why they've not done business with you...the list is only limited by your imagination. The point is this: You could grow your business by 10, 20 or 30% just by adopting an effective e-marketing strategy. Personalize your emails. You want to make sure that your emails stand out from the mass of messages that people find in their inbox. The best way to do this is to personalize your messages. You can either do this manually if you have a fairly small list – or by using one of the many automation systems available. Either way, by including the recipients name, your positive response rate will increase massively.

Summary These are the five biggest mistakes that stop many businesses fulfilling their potential. None of the above is complicated , but by stopping these mistakes and focusing on continually improving your marketing – your business will become much stronger and significantly more profitable.

Chris Cardell - www.CardellMedia.com. You can contact Chris Cardell directly at Chris@CardellMedia.com

With a basic sales process in mind, it's time to move on. There are two specific reasons that I gave you an overview of the reverse-pyramid style of selling in this chapter. First, it's easy. If you can ask questions and get to know people, you can sell anything using this selling style. More importantly though, with its relationship building aspects it fits well with our next Hat – the Hat of servitude.

CHAPTER 8 - THE HAT OF SERVITUDE

In the last chapter we said that nothing happens in business until a sale occurs. In this chapter we're going to put on our service Hat and take that idea a little further. In order for that sale to occur you have to have customers, and serving those customers will be the difference between success and failure.

Notice that I said "will be the difference" and not might be the difference or could be. In any business, customers are its lifeblood. If you have no one to sell to, you are out of business.

Customer service means customer loyalty, and although this chapter isn't the longest in the book by far, understanding the importance of customer service is so important for your business, that I can reasonably state that if you don't work to serve those customers – you will fail. Let's begin our look at customer service with the reasons why customers leave.

The six reasons customers will leave you include:

1. 1% die
2. 3% move away
3. 5% seek alternatives or develop other business relationships
4. 9% begin doing business with the competition
5. 14% are dissatisfied with the product or service
6. 68% are upset with the treatment they've received.

Customer loyalty and the lifetime value of a customer can be worth up to 10 times as much as the price of a single purchase. More importantly, for every complaint a business receives, there are approximately 26 other customers with unresolved complaints or problems.

It gets worse…

A dissatisfied customer will tell up to 10 people about their experience. 13% of those unhappy customers will tell up to 20 people! It could be argued that in this cyber world…one bad experience could take up residency in someone's blog to tell the world how they were slighted.

Building Business 4 Success

. . .

In other words whether you like it or not...**the customer is King**. Another way to put it is with the two rules of customer service:

1. Rule #1 ---The customer is always right.
2. Rule #2 ----When the customer is wrong, refer to Rule 1.

My point here is that your customers matter. Without them you don't even have a business. Remember that customers are...

- The most important people in your business
- Not the interruption of our work...they are the purpose of it
- Part of our business...not outsiders
- Deserving of the most courteous and attentive treatment we can give them.
- The lifeblood of this...and every other business.

We can also look at this from a business stand point. **Gaining a customer may cost as much as 20x the cost of keeping one**. More than that, a happy customer can be your best advertising tool. Word-of-mouth advertising is free, and it brings customers who already trust you before they buy.

What I'm really trying to get at here is that serving your customers matters. Customer service means keeping your customers happy, and working to resolve their issues quickly and effectively. By always keeping the idea that "The Customer is King" in your mind you'll be working to experience growth in the long run. You'll get repeat business, recommendations from happy clients, and you'll spend less money trying to gain new customers than the business down the street.

The main points of keeping customers loyal include:

1. Value – You must offer them value with your product or service.
2. Relationship – A huge part of loyalty comes from getting to know your customers. People are much more likely to buy from someone they know and trust than they are from someone they don't.
3. Product Itself –The product or service you sell also plays into customer service. A good product will be recommended more often than a poor one, and a customer who is happy with your product will be much more likely to buy it again.

Everything from employee morale to your bookkeeping habits can play into the way your customers see you. For example if the customer was initially happy with the sale, but your accounting department took two months to send the bill and then billed the wrong amount – that customer likely isn't going to be a loyal customer.

Customer service doesn't just happen at the time of sale; it's a part of all of the hats you wear. As your business grows, and you have more employees working for you they also become the face of your business. If you're management skills are such that your employees are happy and they like their jobs that will come through when they serve your clients. On the other hand if you treat your employees poorly and they're just sticking around until they find something better – that will also come through when they serve your customers.

When it comes to serving clients in your business you have to ask how you want your customers to view you. There are really only two answers here. **You're either doing an excellent job**, in which case your customers are so impressed some of them do take the time to recommend you. **Or you aren't**, in which case you may as well check off poor on the customer service marks:

What I really want you to gain here is that customer service matters to your success. Also that everything you do in your business, in one way or another, will eventually play into the service you provide to your customers.

CHAPTER 9 - THE FINANCIAL HAT

When it comes to business, keeping track of finances is important. You need to track all sales and expenses and handle your money correctly. It's time to put on your financial Hat and start doing just that.

One of your first jobs was to get an accounting system. Then you need to either do it yourself or get someone to do it for you. Without tracking your sales and expenses not only will you have no idea of where your business is at, but you'll also be setting yourself up for disaster when tax time comes.

This particular Hat, although not necessarily one you will always wear yourself, is very important. You need to have someone you trust to manage your business finances. It won't do to let just anyone manage your books.

Accounting Software

The first thing you are going to need is some accounting software to allow for easy data management. There are a few ways you could go with this step. As I said earlier in the book, I highly recommend QuickBooks.

They aren't the only decent accounting suite out there though, so here are some options to get you started:

1. Intuit QuickBooks – An easy to learn, fully functional, accounting package.
2. PeachTree Accounting – QuickBooks largest competitor, also a good choice.
3. MYOB Accounting – Have a full suite of business software available for many aspects of accounting and business management.
4. Sage Business Vision – Another excellent bookkeeping package that is gaining popularity.
5. Avaquest Bookkeeper – Not as complete as the first four, but very easy to learn and quite inexpensive to get started. May be suitable for home based businesses.

The important thing to ensure when you select an accounting

package is that it contains enough functionality to take care of the books for your business. For most start-ups, one of the accounting packages listed earlier will be more than enough to get you started.

If you find that your business needs a larger suite of features such as CRM (customer relationship management) or ERP (enterprise resource planning) a simple Google search will turn up many companies dedicated to that type of software. There are also software packages tailored to specific industries that may be worth looking at.

For example if you are starting a service oriented business, you will need an accounting package like QuickBooks or MYOB. But there are other tools that will integrate with those programs to make your bookkeeping even easier. A software tool like Field Connect will allow you to manage dispatch and billing in the field, and you'll be able to integrate that data into your main accounting package.

When it comes to managing your money you really just want to ensure two things:

1. Whenever money is involved you keep close track of what is going on.
2. Your bookkeeping is done well enough to be able to give your accountant everything he needs at the end of the year by simply exporting your books.

Both of those items are taken care of by getting a good set of software tools that fits your business, and using them religiously. As an example, if you set up your business with a point-of-sale system that tracks every sale, then no sale should be made without using your POS tool. Setting your business up this way so that your consistent with your processes will ensure keeping your money in order is easy.

Putting on Your Financial Hat

Once you have the software in place that will help you keep track of things you need to actually use it. I wanted to separate this from the software section, because it really is a completely different set of ideas. Your accounting software is a tool to help you keep your books in order. Your financial Hat is the processes you setup to ensure your money is managed correctly.

Many business owners don't wear this particular Hat themselves. They might have a family member do the books, or possibly they hire a bookkeeper or accountant to take care of all of it. What you need to ensure in this case is that whoever you have managing your money is someone you trust.

In my case, my wife took over the responsibility for this job as well as all the admin and office responsibilities. She worked to her strengths: detail work, organization and office filing. And, I worked to my strengths: sales, marketing, and public relations.

There have been many cases where employees who were handling the books and money have embezzled from their employer, so I cannot tell you how important it is to have the right people doing this. In my case, WE always keep this job in the family (my wife, then my oldest son). **Remember, NO ONE CARES LIKE THE OWNER.**

At this point – once you have your accounting software, and know who will take care of the books – you need to put the processes in place to keep them always up to date.

Your books should be complete enough to tell you at any time where your sales are at, how much above/behind you budget you are, etc. This information is important to being able to grow your business and plan for the future. It's also important to give you the information you need to see your successes and failures right now.

CHAPTER 10 - THE LEGAL HAT

The next Hat we need to talk about is the legal Hat. This one will vary a bit depending on the type of business you start, but that doesn't mean it's not important.

Without understanding the legal issues surrounding your business you may be setting yourself up for failure in the form of massive lawsuits or worse – jail time! That may sound harsh, but it is the truth. So without further ado, let's put on our legal Hat and get right into corporate law and your business.

There are really two things you need to be able to wear this Hat well. First you're going to need a corporate lawyer. Then, you're going to need a good understanding of the law as it pertains to your business.

First Things First – Your Attorney

When we start to talk about lawyers, most people get the image of some dishonest chum working to make a living in a courtroom by ripping off those who hire them. In general, lawyers are seen as dishonest and as a profession those who practice law are looked down on by society in general. In fact, public distrust of lawyers was what led to the rise of legal self-help packages in many different areas, including packages that can help you in your own business.

When it comes to your business, this is one of those cases where I do recommend you put that general distrust aside and find a corporate lawyer that you can trust. It will save you time when dealing with legal matters, and it will help to protect you and your business in the long run. A good corporate and legal attorney can assist you in any matters that relate to the business.

I had one from the beginning of each business to help with all the initial corporate and legal matters such as starting the corporation itself or dealing with contracts. Having an attorney available for any questions and problems that **WILL** arise as you build the company is important. Make sure this person is someone you have complete trust in.

. . .

If you need help finding an attorney, and you don't feel the yellow pages are the right place to start, try asking some other local business owners. Most entrepreneurs will be able to recommend a lawyer, because in all likelihood they have had to use the services of one if they've been in business for any length of time at all.

The Law and Your Business

Once you've found a lawyer to help you with legal matters, it's important that you take the time to learn the law as it pertains to your business. Many different industries are regulated by different government bodies, and those industries probably do have laws that will affect you. There can be federal, state, and local laws pertaining to any given type of business. For you as an entrepreneur knowing those laws is important to your own success.

Obviously, I can't cover the law as it pertains to the thousands of different industries out there, but I can give you some resources to get you started.

1. Your Corporate Lawyer – The attorney we talked about in the last section is an excellent resource to learning the law for your business. If they don't know the specific laws for your industry, they will have the resources to find them out for you, and if you use them to start your business they may have already pointed out laws that you need to be aware of.
2. The Internet - A simple Google search will very often turn up federal and state regulations on any given business type. It's also a useful tool for finding any regulatory bodies that govern your industry.

What's important here is that you become aware of anything that may pertain to the way you operate. For example, you wouldn't want to start a restaurant without being familiar with local and state health laws; or, you wouldn't want to start that excavation business without being aware of the laws pertaining to buried pipes and cables. For many industries there are laws specific to that type of business. Knowing them is your first step in protecting yourself.

Protecting Yourself and Your Business

I wanted to end this chapter by giving you one last idea to help protect yourself legally. It's not complicated, but it is important. The idea that I want to share is that as a business owner you need the right type of insurance.

Just because you run your business from your home doesn't mean that you aren't legally liable for things that may arise. For example, that courier who slipped on your icy step and broke his arm can sue you. If the package came in the name of a business, and you didn't let your insurance company know that you were running a business from home then most insurers won't cover it!

When you start your business, get a lawyer, get familiar with the laws pertaining to your industry, and ALWAYS carry enough insurance to protect yourself and your business. By doing all three you'll wear your legal hat well, and you won't have to worry as much about unforeseen legal issues.

CHAPTER 11 - IT'S A CAPITAL HAT!

When it comes to starting your business, one thing you're going to need is capital. That is, money to start your business, and money to keep it going as you get the business off the ground. Remember that lack of capital is one of the main reasons businesses fail, and for that reason we need to talk about your capital Hat.

Most people think of capital as the money needed to start the business. They think of money to buy inventory, to pay for buildings, etc. That is part of the capital you will need, but it isn't all of it. Along with getting your business started you also need to ensure you have enough capital to keep it going until it becomes self-sufficient.

Everything from money to purchase equipment and office furniture to how you're going to pay your monthly bills and finance your inventory must be considered when deciding on how much capital you will need. You also need to budget something for unforeseen expenses. There will likely be some as you are getting started. Having extra money on hand to deal with them will ensure you don't get stuck because of something you didn't think of.

In a previous chapter we talked about your planner's Hat. In that chapter we mostly talked about creating a realistic sales plan, and using that sales plan to ensure you had the money you need to keep the business going.

There are some cases though where a business may not become self-sufficient in its first months in business. What do you do then? And then of course there is raising the money you actually need to start the business itself. Maybe you need $100,000 and you only have $25,000 in savings. Maybe you have no money at all, but you believe your business idea is solid and if you can just start it you will be able to get it making money.

Whatever the case, where are you going to get the additional money you need? How will you cover those expenses if your realistic sales expectations won't cut it for the first month or two? How will you purchase your inventory? What about building rent, the phone bill, and your wages? How much do you need to live?

These are all questions that you should be asking yourself when you are deciding on how much you need to start out. Putting on your capital Hat is both a lesson in planning, and a part of you working towards your own success. Wearing this Hat will be harder for some that for others, but if you believe in the business you are about to start, it's an important part of doing what is needed to get your entrepreneurial journey off the ground.

How Much Capital will You Need

Before we start to discuss how to raise the capital you need, it's important to decide how much you actually need. You could spend months raising the money you thought you needed, but if you didn't raise enough to begin with then you very likely will fail. At the very least, you'll cause yourself problems that could have been avoided.

This particular exercise needn't be difficult but it is important. To get you started let's revisit the example I gave you when we talk about forecasting sales using the rules of 78's:

Month 1	Month 2	Month3
$1282	$2564	$3846
Month 4	Month 5	Month 6
$5128	$6410	$7692
Month 7	Month 8	Month 9
$8974	$10,256	$11,538
Month 10	Month 11	Month 12
$12,820	$14,100	$15,382

Remember that at that point we used the rule of 78's to create a forecast for our sales for the first year of business. Using the example above let's consider for a moment.

For the first month we forecast that we can make $1282 in sales. For the second we have $2564, and for the third we have $3846. What if our monthly obligations for those first three months were more than that?

. . .

Maybe you calculated that you need $2800 per month to meet your personal expenses, and an additional $2500 each month when you're starting out to pay for business expenses such as advertising, office rent, etc. From that example we would need $5300 just to meet our expenses, and our sales forecast says that we won't make that until month 5. In other words when we raise the capital we need to get started we also need to consider the money we need to stay in business for those first 4 months.

It doesn't really matter what the figures are, what does matter is that you account for it when you're starting out. When starting a business most of us put a good deal of our own money on the line. With all of your own money tied up you have to ask yourself: could you afford to be without an income for four whole months?

The answer to that question is probably no, and that's the reason it's so important to bring realistic sales numbers into play when calculating your startup needs.

From all of that we need to calculate the capital we need to start our business based on all of the following:

1. The money **you need to live.**
2. The money needed to meet **monthly business expenses.**
3. The **money required to for startup**. This includes everything from money for land or rent to inventory and office equipment.
4. **Something extra** for the things we missed (and there will be unforeseen expenses that you couldn't have planned for).

The easiest way to calculate a realistic number is to sit down with a piece of paper, or a spreadsheet on your PC, and work it all out. Don't forget to account for those first months, and for every cost involved in getting your business started. As an example:

> *Desk, Chair and PC for Office – $2740*
> *Accounting Software and POS System - $2300*
> *Legal Expenses - $800*
> *Office Rent Month One through Four - $500 x 4 = $2000*
> *Wages (Paying Myself) - $2800 per month x 4 = $10,400*
> *Inventory - $3,400*
> *Advertising - $600 x 4 = $2400*
> *Misc Expenses - $2500*

Obviously the example is simplistic, but you get the idea.

Raising Capital

Once you have a solid number in mind, as to what you need to get going with your business, it's time to talk about how to raise the capital you need. There are many ways to get the money you need for startup. If you are serious about the business you have in mind you will make use of as many of them as you need to and not quit until you have the money you require.

When you're wearing your capital Hat, you'll often be required to play the role of the convincer. That is – you believe in your business, but if you want money from others to start it, then you had better learn how to sell the idea to them as well. Banks, investors, or even your family and friends will usually need a reason to part with their money and invest in your business. The best reason you can give them is to show them how you WILL succeed.

One thing to note here: If you do intend to seek sources such as banks or business loan centers to raise the money you need, you will need a formal business plan before you start.

With that out of the way let's talk about some common ways to raise capital.

Your Money

If you have savings, investments, other properties besides your home, or some other money tucked away somewhere then obviously that is the simplest way for you to start. By using your own money you needn't worry about paying back loans, or being tied to anyone else when you start your business.

If you have everything you need to get started then you need to look no further. Start your business and move on to the next Hat. Many people, however, won't have all of the money they require and will need to seek help from outside sources.

Friends and Family

Maybe you aren't rolling in cash at the moment, but do you know someone who is? A friend, a relative, or a family member can all be sources of capital when you start your business.

If you use this method of raising capital be sure to have a formal contract written that includes how and when the money will be paid back and the terms of the loan. This will help you to keep money and your relationship separate and can save misunderstandings and ruined relationships.

THE FAINTEST INK IS WORTH MORE THAN THE FONDEST MEMORY!!!!

In other words PUT IT IN WRITING! Don't do anything verbally!

The Bank(s)

As mentioned earlier, you need to establish a banking relationship with someone that you can work with in the future growth of you business. Along with starting your business accounts, your bank may also be an excellent place to go to raise the money you need to get started.

I would suggest you stay away from big banks and look for a local small business oriented bank that shows interest in what you are doing.

Make sure they have business credit cards you can get to use for paying expenses and vendors. Also, make sure that they have merchant services that will provide you credit card services you can use for your customers to use on your website to buy your products or services.

Even if you don't seek money from the bank, building a relationship with your banker is very important. It will become very critical to the growth of your business and your banker can become your partner, albeit unwittingly, in getting you working capital and cash flow for the company both now and as your business grows.

Investors

Another way to raise capital is by seeking investors. Many financiers will work with entrepreneurs to help them get their businesses off the ground, and these types of investors can finance part, or all, of your startup costs.

If you seek capital in this way you should decide ahead of time what you're willing to give in return. Some investors will seek interest as payment, much like a bank, but others will want share in your business and/or partial control of your operations.

Again with this type of loan be sure to get your lawyer involved and keep everything clearly stated and legal so that you don't end up with terms you didn't know you agreed to.

Other Ways to Raise Capital

The methods of raising capital that I listed thus far are just the most common. They aren't by any means the only ways to raise the money you need. Some businesses may be financed through other methods such as grants from the government. If you started a franchise some franchisors will also finance your startup costs.

However you raise the money you need, just be sure that everything is legal and in **WRITING**, that you understand the terms, and that you aren't starting out so cash-strapped that you're doomed to fail before you even begin. Paying attention to these elements, when you wear your capital Hat, will ensure that your business gets the right start!

CHAPTER 12 - THE RETIREE'S HAT

Some who read this Book may think that retirement isn't necessarily one of the Hats of business. If you are one of those then I respectfully disagree, and I want to let you know that this is one Hat you should be familiar with right from the start. The retiree's Hat should be the long-term goal that you set for yourself, and planning for retirement should be included right from the start.

It doesn't matter if you're 21 right now or 65. In all cases, your business will be your income for now and your road to retirement, as it was for me. The best thing you can do for the future is to make the present your #1 goal.

What you do today will go a long way toward your retirement and estate planning. Maybe for your first six months in business, you can't fit the extra money in to put aside for your retirement.

If you make that decision then that's okay; even if you did decide to start putting money away for retirement a year or two after you start your business, it should be a part of your original plan, and it should be one of your goals in the long term.

I'm not going to spend a lot of time on this particular Hat, but I do want to suggest to you that retirement planning is an important part of your business. I also want to suggest some simple things that you can do to start wearing this Hat right from the start. Taking the time to fit this into your plan now will ensure that when you do retire – when you are finished putting in the long hours that it takes to grow your business – you have something to show for your life of hard work.

Some things you can do during your working life are:

- Set up a savings account. Put away something each paycheck. Use that account to create an investment portfolio in mutual funds and more.

Retirement planners suggest that putting away 10% of the money you earn is the way to retire well. Someone who starts this in their 30's will be a millionaire by the time they retire.

- Set up a 401K program for your company and employees. This is a very good way to invest in your future. It's also an excellent way to build employee loyalty. By investing in your future you are setting yourself up for retirement, by investing in your employees future you're helping yourself to build a team of loyal employees.

- Have the business provide you with a vehicle, cell phone, Bonuses—things like that.

- Invest in Real Estate, or other assets that will bring long-term returns.

As I stated earlier, this book isn't on retirement planning so I'm not going to take my suggestions much further than that. What I do want you to take with you is that planning for the future is important – right from the start.

In all cases, remember to ENJOY THE JOURNEY, NOT THE DESTI-NATION! YOU HAVE A UNIQUE OPPORTUNITY TO HELP

OTHERS WHEN YOU HAVE YOU OWN BUSINESS, SO MAKE IT A FAMILY ATMOSPHERE.

In our businesses, we have people who have been with us for over 20 years. The average tenure of all the employees in our company is 15 years. Loyalty is your most important attribute as it relates to your employees.

CHAPTER 13 - THE LEARNER'S HAT

Another Hat that you should learn to wear well is the Hat of continuing education – or the learner's Hat as I like to refer to it. This particular Hat is as important to you as start your business as the Hat of knowledge, but it doesn't stop there. By wearing your learning Hat as you go along you'll take your business further, and you'll stay on track for success for years to come.

Remember that all this can do for you is make your time much more productive. You can do more jobs, sell more products, and make more money/profit.

The learning Hat applies to:

- Job Knowledge- Stay on top of cutting edge technology to make your job easier and more productive.
- Tech changes in your industry- Computer hardware and software and other things to make you more productive in the business.

In 2000 after 12 years in business, we could no longer grow or manage the business effectively. The only thing we could do was to stay where we were in size, or make a technological change to allow us to grow effectively.

We made the choice to make the change, and over the next 2 years built our own software program that allowed us to effectively go paperless throughout the entire company. This one change took us from a difficult management situation to a completely secure, safe and paperless system that allowed management to run the company from any computer, anywhere at any time.

We are now the largest company in the US in our industry. We have the ability to not only control our business destiny, but our industry destiny. An independent time motion study showed that we increased productivity by 70% in the field, 50% in the branch offices, and 34% in corporate.

- Sales and Marketing innovations: How can you do a better job getting customers?

We did a lot of one on one meetings and personal visits to build confidence. In our business there are no contracts. It is strictly a relationship business.

Continued learning is an investment in your business and its growth.

It may take the form of seminars, courses, meetings, watching your competitors, and even just learning from experience. It can also be considered learning when you come up with new ways to do things better than you did before. The more you know about the industry you work in the more successful you will be.

When it comes to wearing the learner's Hat, you'll also sometimes take on the role of the teacher. Continued learning shouldn't just be limited to you. It should also be a part of your plan for all of those who work with you.

Training programs for employees can also help you take your business further. These could take the form of industry standard training, or you could develop a whole new training program to help grow your own business. Anything that takes your knowledge, or the knowledge of your employees, further falls under the learning Hat.

This particular Hat should be a part of your business right from day one. Being the best in any industry starts with knowing more and doing it better than any of your competitors ever have. With this idea in mind let's move on to our next hat – the spy's Hat!

CHAPTER 14 - THE SPY'S HAT

The last Hat we need to cover is the Hat of the spy. In this case we aren't really talking about private eye stuff or commercial espionage. The spy's Hat simply refers to knowing your competition.

By knowing who your competition is, what they do, what products/services they offer, how those products compare to yours, and how they operate you'll not only be giving yourself the information you need to beat them in the market, but you'll gain a better understanding of the industry in general. This particular Hat isn't difficult to wear, but it's important to wear it before you ever start your own business.

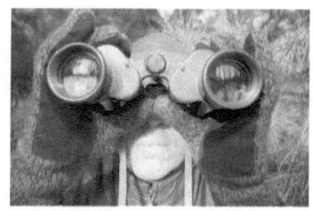

It is always a good idea to know what your competitors are up to. It will help you to stay ahead of your competition and better manage your company. Look for innovative things that you can pick up from them. Look in your industry for things that will make it better and more productive. Then see about making changes.

I remember that when I started in business, I joined local organizations to meet those in the local industry. I also called the bigger competitors to introduce myself. I made it a goal to find out as much as I could about my local market area and who were the big players and why.

Then I proceeded to make every effort to give my customers a better experience than my competition provided and I always ask for referrals. I proceeded to give them exceptional customer service, etc. etc.

Knowing Your Competition

This particular Hat is difficult to wear. In fact, there are simple things you can do to get to know your competition before you ever start your own business. There are also easy ways to keep up on them after you are in business.

The Spy's Hat before You Start Your Business

1. Shop at Your Competitors – Before you go into business simply shopping around in the market you plan to work in is an easy way to find out what it's like to be a customer of your future competition.
2. Past experience – Many people who go into business do so in

markets they already work in. If your new business will be in the same area that you used to work. Think about your employer and how they do things; think about what your customers said about the competition.
3. Trade Magazines – If you work in an industry that has publications specific to your field, subscribe to every trade magazine you can. These types of publications can provide a wealth of information on how others do things. They're also an excellent source of info to find new and better supplies and to keep current with happenings in the industry.
4. Ask Others – If you are starting your business in a specific region, the people who live in that region are an excellent source of information on most businesses in the area. Ask people you know in the area if they've ever dealt with the competition and what their experience was when they did.

Other things you should pay attention to as you're planning your business are things like location, business hours, etc. Whatever you can learn about your future competitors will give you an edge and help you to start your business by doing things better than anyone else in the area does.

The Spy's Hat after You're in Business

Once you are in business there are simple things you can do to stay on top of the competition. Along with the ideas I shared earlier, you might want to:

1. Introduce Yourself – Get to know the other business owners in the area by introducing yourself. Some probably won't be happy that they have a new competitor in the market, but knowing who you are competing with is important.

2. Join Business Associations – If there are associations related to your industry join them. These can be an excellent method of getting to know your competitors both locally and a far.
3. Listen to Your Customers – Many times customers who are new to your business will have dealt with the competition. Listen to the things they say about their past experiences. Whether they are complaining about the competitor or pointing out how they have you beat, this information is important to them, so it should be important to you.

Staying on top of what's happening in the marketplace does include knowing your competitor. This simple act in researching the competition will take you farther in your own business.

When it Comes to Your Competitors…

One last thing that needs to be covered when scoping out your competitors are a few things that you shouldn't do. Too many new business owners go into business with the idea that the best way to compete is by starting out doing things better than the local competitors. Of course this is true, but there are some things you should avoid doing.

When you are just starting out, your business is new to the area, it's quite possible you're working with borrowed funds, and you don't have the customer base that your competitors have worked to gain. This is important to keep in mind.

Your competitors have been in business longer than you, they likely have more working capital than you do, and their expenses will be less (not necessarily less, but they will be covered by the sales they are already making or they wouldn't still be in business). From that let's talk about a hypothetical situation.

Imagine for a second:

> *You've taken the time to scope out your competitors, and you see a couple of ways to beat them right from the start. First, your three big competitors all have offices that are off the beaten path. Your first idea to do things better is to get an office in a better location – right on the main street where customers will have an easier time finding you.*
>
> *Next, you see that two of your competitors charge more for their services than you had originally intended to charge. To gain a larger portion of their customer base you decide to undercut them on their pricing, and actively seek out their current customers by being cheaper and closer to home.*

Now let's talk about what you've just done.

You found a better location for your office. This could be a good thing, maybe you'll gain more customers because of it. But, did you stop to ask yourself why all of your competitors were in offices off the beaten path? Possibly the rent was cheaper and the location didn't affect their business as much as you thought it would?

The answer to those questions will be specific to the business you are starting, but if you didn't ask them to begin with you could possibly be paying $1,000 a month for office rent when your three biggest competitors are paying half that.

Next you decided to undercut them on pricing...Are you seeing what I'm getting at here? You're quite possibly setting yourself up for disaster. Right from the start your expenses are higher and you are earning less. It gets worse though.

Remember the completion has been around for a while. They have an established business and a current customer base. Their expenses are lower, and by going directly at their customers they decide you are a threat. So they lower their prices and undercut you...

Now what do you do? You have enough working capital to make it for a few months, but can you really afford a price war with a business that's been around for years and very likely has a much larger bank roll? Of course you can't.

My point here is simply that knowing your competition is about knowing them so that you can build your business to be stronger and better. It isn't necessarily about going head-to-head with them right from the start. In some cases, as in the example I gave, going directly at your competitors when you are just starting out can be disastrous.

CHAPTER 15 – PUTTING IT ALL TOGETHER – YOUR BUSINESS, YOUR FUTURE

Well here we are. Over 14 chapters we've covered many different aspects of business, and guess what – it's time to talk about how it all fits together. By understanding the information you've been given thus far, you do have the knowledge that is required to be a successful entrepreneur.

So - what's next?

The answer is simple – start your business and start working towards your own success. In fact, the single most important idea that I can teach you is **"Start your business."** Don't procrastinate, don't just dream about it. Learn the 12 hats of business and then just start. This is the single most important step to separating you from the millions of others who only dream about owning their own business.

You have the knowledge you need, you've been working to learn the 12 Hats of business (or will be now) – **just start**. There is one last thing I want to cover before you do.

Let's talk about how everything fits together to make you a successful entrepreneur. We covered 12 areas of business, and we referred to each one as a Hat. The idea being that you will need to switch Hats often as you work to build your business.

By understanding the different roles you may be required to take as a business owner, and working to take on those roles as required, you'll be working towards your own success right from the start.

Let's quickly recap the 12 Hats you should be ready to wear on your entrepreneurial journey:

- **Job Knowledge** – *Industry knowledge will help you to get the right start in your business. In this case, as much as this Hat is about knowing as much as you can about it single role in your business, it's also about knowing the industry in general.*

- **Business Management/Administration** – *As a business owner* *you need to be aware of the management and administration tasks that will be needed, and you need to work to ensure they are done. With the managers Hat, I gave you your first administration tasks and suggested ways that you can become a better manager in the long run.*

- **Technical/Computers** – *Your technical Hat is simply understanding the role that technology will play in your business, and ensuring you gain the skills to suit.*

- **Planning-** *Short and Long Term – You'll need to wear your planner's Hat often as you are beginning to start your business. It isn't just about planning now though. The planner's Hat is also about planning for the future, and always ensuring that your plans are adaptable as the situation requires.*

- **Sales and Marketing** – *Without sales, there is no business. When you put on your sales Hat, you are working towards your success by earning revenue for the company and ensuring your business is more than just a dream.*

- **Customer Service, Customer Service, Customer Service** – *When you wear the Hat of servitude, you are working to build customer loyalty. You know that "The customer is king" and that they are the most important people in your business.*

- **Accounting and Finance** – *When you don your financial Hat, you are working towards your own success by ensuring your finances are in order and your money is safe. You may not always take on this role yourself, but even when you don't you will take the time to ensure that your finances are dealt with by someone you trust.*

- **Legal and Corporate** – *When you wear your legal Hat you are working to protect yourself and your business. Simple things like ensuring you understand that contract before you sign, and carrying the right insurance will keep your business growing without being bogged down in legal issues.*

- **Banking and Working Capital** – *Your capital Hat is about ensuring you have enough working capital to stay afloat. In the beginning this is a calculation you did when planned your business, but you also need to ensure you have money on hand to deal with issues as your business grows.*

- **Retirement and Estate Planning** – *When you put on the retiree's Hat, you aren't just leaving the business behind. In fact, by putting on this Hat early and planning for retirement you are ensuring that the business you are starting now gives you the financial security you desire in the future.*

- **Continuing Education** – *As a business owner you'll be putting on your learning Hat often. Continuing to stay on top of every* aspect of your industry will help you to keep your business on top, and to keep it growing well into the future.

- **Know your Competition** – *Finally you will wear the spy Hat quite often as you are starting out. This will give you the information you need to start your business by doing things better than the competition. It doesn't stop there though, as your business grows you should always be aware of what the competition is doing, and you should be ready to improve your own business to stay on top.*

By simply understanding these 12 elements of business, you do have what it takes to succeed. Start your business, and understand that as a business owner your role will sometimes change. As you need to change your Hat and move on, always work to grow, to learn, to be better than the competition, and you will build a successful business!

To Your Success,

Walt Camping

www.ingramcontent.com/pod-product-compliance
Lightning Source LLC
Chambersburg PA
CBHW021834170526
45157CB00007B/2797